Edited by Faye A. Fields

Published by
Leading Through Living Community, LLC

Copyright 2016 The Distinctive Design of Norahs Khan
by Norahs Khan
Copyright 1991 Diary of Expressions by Norahs Khan
Copyright 1992 Captions of Love by Norahs Khan
Copyright 1992 Obstacles by Norahs Khan
Copyright 1995 Approach... If You Dare
Copyright 1996-2000 By Way of A Ray of Sunlight
Individual copyright reserved by artists as indicated.

All rights reserved. Written permission must be secured from the author to use or reproduce any part of this book.

INTRODUCTION

May these heartfelt expressions
nestle inside a safe place and bring
you comfort in knowing
you are not alone.

Thankful for this healing journey.

Breathe

Dedication

To Divine Light,
without you I am not.

To Ryan, my great niece, may you continue your path with the same spirit of strength as you demonstrated upon arrival.

To Isaiah, my nephew, your creativity brings me inspiration every time I hear your outstanding contributions. May you continue to touch lives and uplift with your excellence.

To the woman who introduced me to a woman who changed my life.

BOOK I:
DIARY OF WRITTEN EXPRESSIONS

1991

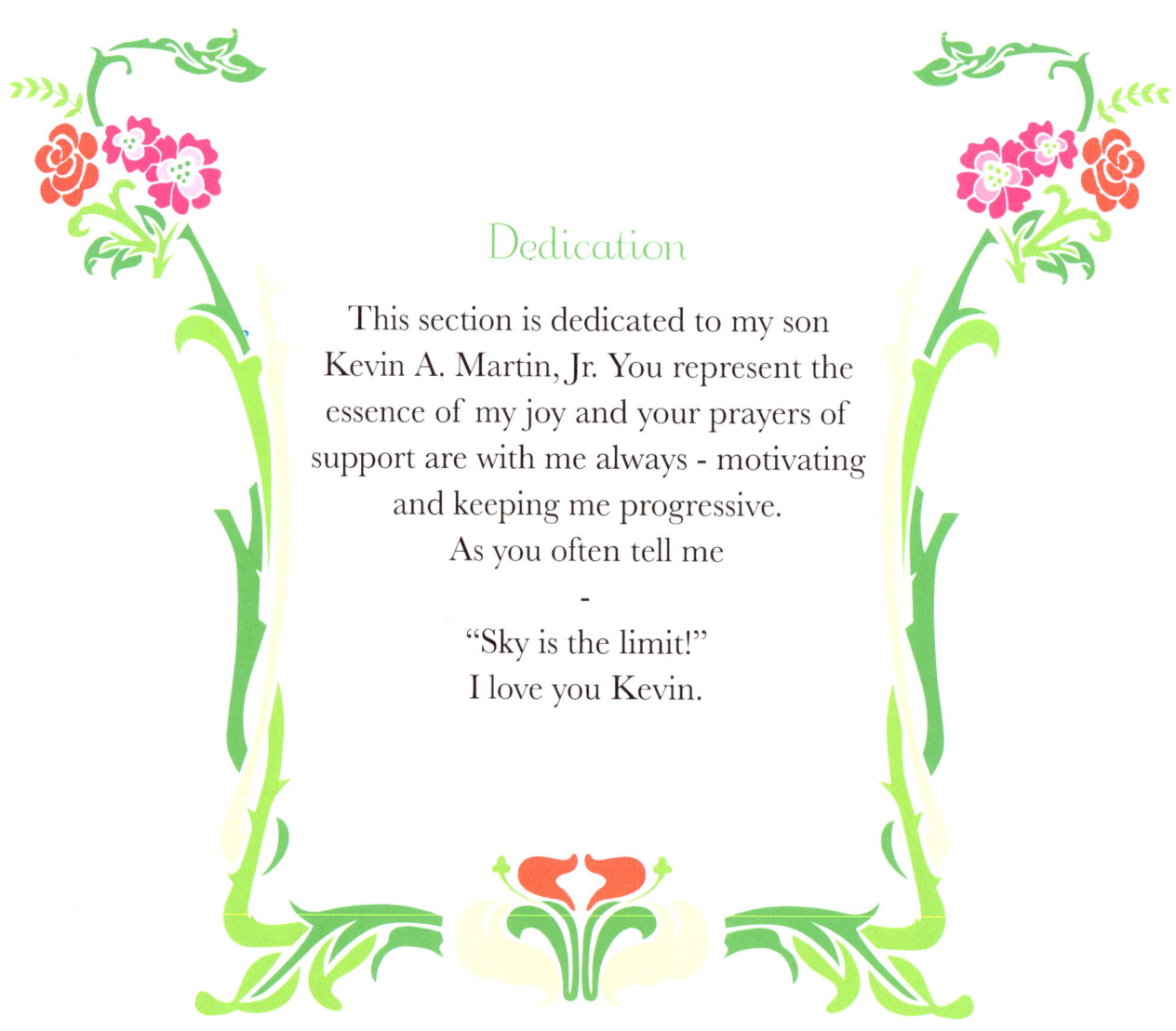

Dedication

This section is dedicated to my son Kevin A. Martin, Jr. You represent the essence of my joy and your prayers of support are with me always - motivating and keeping me progressive.
As you often tell me
-
"Sky is the limit!"
I love you Kevin.

**Special thanks to God
for my gift with words to share with all.**

Appreciation to Frank Tucker III, Linda Leggett, Nathaniel Clark, Kendryck Victor C. Allen, Luis Torres and all those warm hearts that graciously shared and supported me to make my dream a reality.

INTRODUCTION

"Diary of Written Expressions" provides a comfort level for feelings of desire. My poems convey messages of love, pain, inspiration and passion as they arouse your senses. I share heartfelt emotions with sincere respect to my personal experiences. My view on love and happiness inspires positive ideas and reveals painful realities.

Often, we experience a feeling or desire that securely remain inside ourselves. We fear revealing our hearts and souls to others. The phobia of rejection masters our actions at some point in our lives. When I began to share my intimate poetry - I discovered I can reach an inner-core of myself through the relationship of my written expressions and people who receive my messages. This discovery sparked radiance in my heart and motivation to continue creative expressions.

"Diary of Written Expressions" provides a basis from which I can convey various emotions of strength, weakness, pain, and love. Thank you for sharing with me.

MESSAGES OF LOVE

Inside...
Inside my heart is your love
Inside our soul is your spirit
Inside my life you are welcome
I love you

Vision
Close your eyes
Feel me caressing your body, tenderly
Appreciate the softness and warmth
You behold in your hands
Taste my lips in your mouth
Wet and delicious
They quiver with anticipation
Smell our body scents blend naturally
As we motion to become one
See my eyes surrender all
Hear my gentle whispers
Sincerely, I say "I Love You"

In My Heart You Remain

Because of you...
There's a feeling embracing my soul
Such a grip
I can't control
The power of love inspires my yearning
I tried to hold back
But, everyday I'm learning
It is a complicated situation
For which I've not found
A resolution
One day, perhaps I'll learn to
Master the game
Until then my love
In my heart you remain

Benefit of Our Love

As my body yearns for your touch
My softness pulsates with desire
The aroma of love is in the air
I imagine you watching me
As my quivering thighs wait
To engage you inside my
Comforting thickness
I see the pleasure in your
Eyes as we gently blend
And you are surrounded
By my love
Entangled bodies,
Rhythmic motions
"Oh Yes" I whisper
"This is the benefit of
Our love"

Memories Between A Lady and A Man

How sweet the memories
Of our beginning together
That precious time shared
With laughter and your gentle touch
We knew then our special way
Would last forever
I told you "I love you"
Now - you know how much
We've made adjustments
And we cope
Always keeping the sweetness
Of the memories close to our hearts
Both of us keep strong with hope
As we return to the comfort
Of each others' arms
Thought the year apart
We begin to understand
The sweetness of the memories between
A lady and a man

To The One I Love

It is my pleasure
To share this special time of year
With the one I love
You are the one that cares
And holds me dear in heart
You are the one that restores
My strength and replenishes
My soul when things fall apart
Your gift from deep inside
So tender and sweet
Has tantalized my desire to
Feel complete
Your love I protect and accept
With a precious embrace
Remember this for now
And for always
I love you

MESSAGES OF INSPIRATION

A Thought

Time doesn't slow down for us
We are responsible and accountable
For our own accomplishments
Therefore, we must conquer
All we can

How Fortunate

Changes in my life
Seemingly grim
Leading me through the destine path
To discover
How fortunate I really am

Positive Outcome

Sometimes my future seems gray
I must keep strong everyday
There is no crime
To complete my time
And get the opportunity
To take my place in society
Then everyone will know and see
That I can be the best for me
Looking forward to that moment
When all will be done
Keeping my head high
For a positive outcome

Your Gift of Caring

You thought to call me today
So comforting to know
That you think about me
Please don't let go
Your gentle words
Bring pleasure to my heart
I've noticed the absence
When we are apart
I welcome the excitement
To know you'll come again
The joy is refreshing
And well accepted
Your gift of caring
Is the best kind of medicine

Never A Doubt

Sometimes my thoughts
Easily transforms into perfect words
But then there are times
When I can't express
How I'm feeling inside
Even though confusion may surface
In our lives
My love for you
Is never a doubt

 # MESSAGES OF MISSING YOU

Someday Soon
Beholding the gentleness of your caress
And the sweetness of your kiss
The memories intensify
With each passing sun
My strong desire for more
Is overpowering
Let us share all we feel
Someday Soon

Wishes
One day...
If only...
Maybe... But -
However, I Love You

Let's make up

The Moment

Waiting to see you again has aroused me
My thoughts of us together are visual
I imagine how you'll touch me
Where you'll touch me
Your hands gently holding my face
As you slowly motion forward
To give my lips the softness of yours
The closeness of our bodies has motivated
Our spirits with strong desires to make
This feeling last
I feel you breathing as you lift
Me up into your embrace
As we both gaze pleasurably
Into each other's eyes
We assure ourselves -
Yes, this is the moment

MESSAGES OF REACHING OUT

Surrender

I want to know
How to satisfy your mind
How to fulfill your soul
How to warm your heart
Surrender
Grant me the chance

I Needed to Be Understood

You saw how sad I was
My tears were cold and plentiful
Deep inside - my pain endless
A warm touch or friendly smile
A shoulder - if I could...
I needed to be understood

Intrigue

Our first encounter was brief
Yet the anticipation of seeing you
Has excited all my emotions
I wonder who you are inside
Why am I so drawn to you
How powerful your language
Both physical and mental
You have stirred desire
With such intrigue

Your Special Way

Our eyes locked from across the room
Your message received and well understood
I replied positively in your direction
So smooth in motion - absolute connection
Your personable quality
Flirted with my curiosity
Our conversation revealed
A pleasant and refined gentleman
Frustrations in my life have been a true test
Charismatic charm you do possess
Your sensitivity is steady and comforting
You are indeed set apart from the rest
Plenty to say about your special way
You choose to share your kind way
Thank you, for the support
And encouragement
It means so much to have a dear friend

Our Moments

As we sit alone
Thinking of our moments
Shared together
I smile inside and out with delight
Knowing how much closer each moment
Has brought our spirits
You have somehow penetrated
The depths of my emotions
Emotions that have been dormant
For a long time
I want this good feeling to last

My Tears of Pain

Deep inside, I'm so alone
Sadness and disbelief
I search for the answers
No one understands my grief
Kind words and friendly gestures
Provide temporary relief
Soon I'll face the emptiness
The cycle never ends
yearning for the last hour
The essence of my life is hopelessness
Something is missing
The void is deep
Oh Lord my sanity
I wish to keep
I cry out loud
Sometimes I cry in silence
All strength seems drained
From my tears of pain

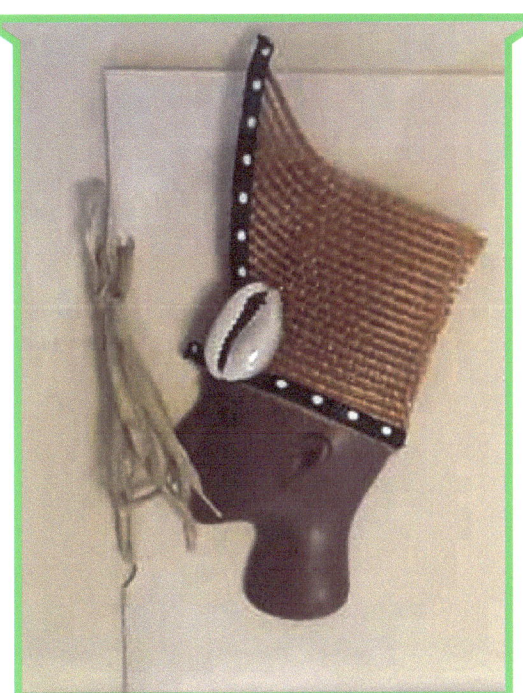

When We Met
When we met
I loved you from the start
You won me over easy
With your endearing heart
Your strength and guidance
Gave me confidence to pursue
My uninhibited nature
Sometimes surprised you
Although apprehensive you said
"Yes"
Thank you, Mom
For the chance to reflect me best

No Matter How Far

So small this miracle
I behold in my arms
A new kind of love felt deep inside
I define as innocence and pride
As you grow, time passes quickly
Many changes occur
We adjusted with dignity
So young in years
The pressure seemed great
Faith and love keep us tough
We have not time for hate
As we continue in life
You remain supportive
No need to be timid
You always tell me -
"No matter how far, Mom
Sky is the limit"

Sorry My Love

Thinking about the time we shared
Laughter and tears
You knew from the start I was scared
Erasing all my fears
You said, "Everything would be fine"
I couldn't resist
You were so kind
The treatment was special and sweet
No one could compete
Passion and pain
Things didn't remain the same
I had to let go
Even though you said, "No"
Always remember
You are in my heart
Sorry, My Love
You and I must part
Perhaps someday you'll face the pain
Soon I hope there is so much to gain

BOOK II:
CAPTIONS OF LOVE

1992

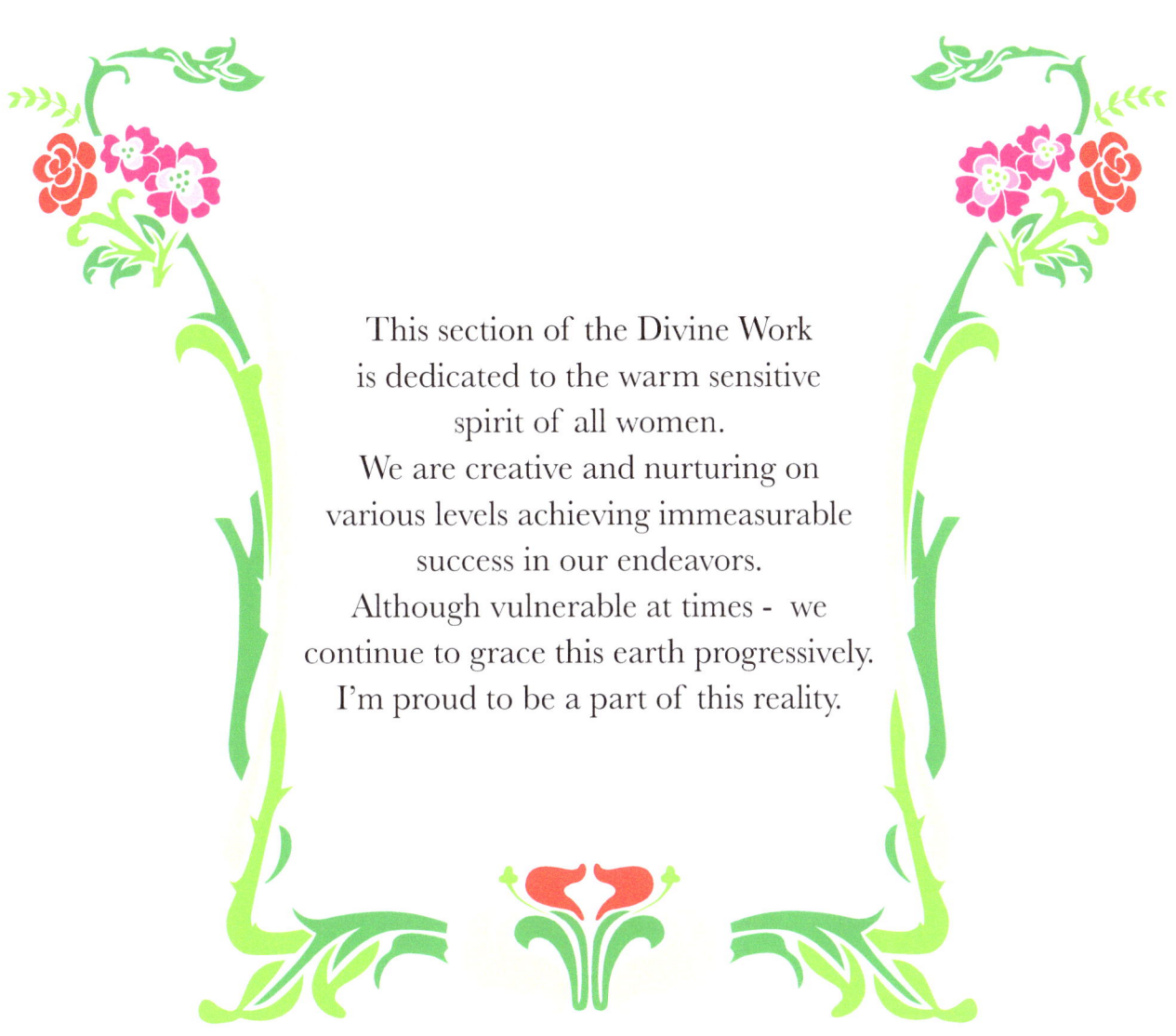

This section of the Divine Work
is dedicated to the warm sensitive
spirit of all women.
We are creative and nurturing on
various levels achieving immeasurable
success in our endeavors.
Although vulnerable at times - we
continue to grace this earth progressively.
I'm proud to be a part of this reality.

INTRODUCTION

Captious Love embraces you comfortably
as you explore your feelings of love
and desire. Passionate messages boldly
conveyed to you while stirring emotions
as they stimulate your mind.
Moods of excitement
and intrigue seize you and allow your
imagination to experience a visual
journey as your eyes absorb each word.

Creativity is more than fun -
it grants me a level of power to
develop a thought and present
this thought to you - bringing pleasure
to your heart through your eyes.

I'm sharing with you an opportunity to escape into Captious Love.
The intensity of passion appeals to your curiosity and you will find
it irresistible and want me.

MOODS OF INTRIGUE

Free Me

Enter me through the passages
Of sensual pleasures
I embrace the sensation of love
As the warmth of our closeness
Intoxicate my existence
Absorb the energy surrounding our oneness
Penetrate my innocence
Razzle my urges
Stimulate my desire
Free me, I'm yours

Your Eyes

Congenial signals aggressing my senses
As we engage curiously
Sparking purposeful impulses
As we indulge immeasurably
Our connection endless
As we entangle progressive intimacy
Seizing my control
As we endure intensely
Captured by the mirror of your soul
Your eyes possess a fine quality

Casual Encounter

Sleep and appealing
Drawn by your inviting smile
Interested in dealing
Oh yes, I like your style
Rendezvous at eight
We were both on time
Tender strokes
You are gentle and kind
You excite my senses
I know we never meant this
Feelings getting stronger
What can I do
Now that I've fallen for you
During a casual encounter

Shadows

As the sweet scented candle burns
The delicate fragrance fills the air
Moods of love - we yearn
Come close to me, I dare

Playful yet eager - you tease
My love waiting and wanting to please
In the dimmest of light
Intense passion in flight

We gently become one
As our excitement surges high
Our eyes reveal all
Watching the shadows on the wall

Render A Paradise

I want to...
calm your fears and quiet your tears
I want to...
embrace your plight with my love, so tight
I want to...
encourage you with hope
and render a paradise for security
a utopia, to cope
I want to...
elaborate your dreams
and nourish your desires
I want to...
seek our true purpose
and discover and endeavors
I want to...
assure stability
and celebrate our victory

Magnetize My Love

Engage my soul -
with your tender rapture
Excite my passion gently
I want to rave of this capture
Impress my sensitivity
with since affection
Liberate my heart - and
magnetize my love
in your direction

MOODS OF STIMULATION

Looking Through Innocent Eyes…
So lovely and warm
I see
So gentle - you are to me
You glow with hue of excitement
and all the beautiful colors
of the rainbow
Your smile is cheerful
and I like being around you so -
Hearing your words, they inspire me
to express the deep thoughts inside me
You give me the extra something - I need
and now I feel complete
So lovely and warm
I see
So gentle you - you are to me
I'm captured by your presence -
While looking through innocent eyes

My Forever Love

I don't know why...
I think about our love
It's distant now
The years and miles separate
our paths
But our mutual love will truly last
So intense - my memories
of our passion together
I love so much -
Nothing can sever
the bonds of our spirits
connected always
Our hearts know
the impact of it all
My thoughts continue
as I stare at the wall
Now I know why
I went through it all...
You are my forever love

…Just A Little While
Embrace me close
and
Warm my chill of fear
Gently kiss my sadness
With deep understanding
Patiently - allow my distant way
Secure me - tenderly
With your promising smile
Share your strength -
For just a little while

Thoughts I Can't Erase
I Desire...
To resist the force
that disciplines my nature
To caress the warmth
of your love
To explore my passion
as you observe, my behavior
Holding , Touching
Below and Above
To arouse your senses
with my tenderness
To surround you with
infinite rapture and happiness
To softly stroke
your sensitivity
To exceed my dreams
of pleasure and ecstasy
To know the security
of your tight embrace
These thoughts of you,
I can't erase

High Intensity

Your eyes dark and gentle -
They reach my soul
Your tender soft kisses down
My back - please me
As I pretend to escape
And you gain control
Your caress secures me in place
As your words ravish my mind
Your caring smile -
Reflects the love
You have for me
My heart beats fast -
With high intensity

When

When my smile invites
you by my side
...my embrace
brings promise
...my eyes reveal
your thoughts
Then - you'll know
WHEN

If I Were the Sky

If I were the sky
you would be my warm glowing sun
and my gorgeous blue hue
with soft fluffy clouds
to begin my day

If I were the sky
you would be my smooth black velvetiness
and the distinct twinkle in my brilliant stars
granting all wishes

you would be my radiant moon
casting light through my darkness
and inspiring the grace of movement
upon the waters of the world
with your cool windy splendor
to complete my day

If I were the sky
you would share
all my beauty

MOODS OF TRUTH

Control the Destiny

I want to understand
the right way to love you
I thought it all out
a few years back

Obviously I'm off track

Tell me
Teach me
Guide me through
To your soul

How may I know
What's in store
Embrace my desire
To know you more

Control the destiny
Of our unity

They Say
THEY SAY...
"I'm sure you have a special someone"
"I know your phone rings off the hook"
"I'm sure your calendar is full"
"He's a lucky guy"
"I know this weekend, you'll have lots to do"

I just smile politely
And think to myself

If only it were true

I AM

Someone who wants to share
dreams and realities

Someone who cries at joyful moments
and painful memories

Someone who wants a friend
to turn to

Someone who wants to know she
is special to you

Someone who knows pain and sorrow
but more - I endure

Someone who wants to give your life
new meaning with good taste

Someone who enjoys the warmth
of a sincere embrace

Someone with passions raging
inside because they can not
yet be released

I am a lady, a woman with a locked heart
that aches for the one with the key

Why Ask Why

To Soothe You -

I'll prepare your bath
at just the right temperature
with added softeners and fragrance

To Comfort You -

I'll massage you
with sweet oil and
gentle hands

To Secure You -

I'll whisper my thoughts
of love -
as I hold you close

To Protect You -

I'll share your pain
and lighten your burden
with sincere understanding

Message of Promise

After you left -
the images of your
words remained

I imagined clearly
how gentle you would be
After our talk -
I can see
that
things between us
can't ever be the same

I know
from your heart
your words came

Afterthoughts all over my mind
your mental touch is so kind
your caress indeed very tender
dare I - continue to hinder
or should I simply surrender

After your message of promise????????????

Just for Being Me
Once I reserved a
place for you
in my life
I sincerely felt we could
be a powerful force

But
Your attitude soon
changed that course
I was crushed with
disbelief
disappointment
and
suffered much grief

The empty space
you left behind
Has been filled with
Someone - so gentle and kind

I now know how
powerful a force can be
To be loved
Just for being me

MOODS OF PASSAGE

Circumstance

I thought to call you today
There is so much to say

Miss your laugh
and the twinkle in your eyes

Miss your special way
you show how you care

I wanted to tell you
what is in my heart
and how I feel
when we are apart

I thought to call you today
when I passed by your picture
I took a glance

I couldn't call you today
because of our unfortunate circumstance

I Miss You

I'm thinking of
Our SPECIAL LOVE
A wondrous feeling
completely surrounding me
Below and above
Energizing my existence
With joy and pleasure
Your love flow
Has no measure
Freely -
We indulged ourselves
Absorbing all -
Ignoring the signs
Of our fall
We pursued
Our SPECIAL LOVE
Through and through
Now you are gone
And
I MISS YOU

However

I DON'T NEED YOU TO...
play in my hair
or
tell me you care
serve me breakfast in bed
or
help plan my future ahead
share in my spiritual growth
or
pick me up when I'm feeling low
suggest long walks
or
share special talks
HOWEVER -
The above is your clue
and
I WANT YOU TO

If I Could Have It My Way

If I could have it my way
I'd like for you to stay
I'd like to converse
and share -
Enjoy each moment
you show how you care -
Escape into a world
with just you and I
If I could have it my way
I'd show how much
I LOVE YOU
Til I die

No Longer

Your words
were cold and hurtful
Our actions
were unfamiliar and defensive
Our relationship
has suffered immensely
I have learned
that my imperfections
are not acceptable
to you --
I've decided to no longer
live in accordance
to your approval --

Thank You

Because of you
I'm stronger
The shoulder I never had
I need no longer
Although, it took me time
To see -
I understand we were
Never meant to be
I've had much time to think
While we were apart
I'm free from the pressures
To capture your heart
As our lives separate
I wish you well
My thoughts of you
Will deeply dwell

Thank You

Now, I'm stronger
Your shoulder - I never had
I NEED IT NO LONGER

No Call

Again - Waiting
I THOUGHT
you were coming to visit
me today
I THOUGHT
you told me on the phone
you will call
YOU DON'T NEED TO EVER AGAIN
WASTE MY TIME OR YOURS!!!

I don't deserve this treatment
I don't know why I stood for it all
YOU,
YOUR LIES
AND
NO CALL

You Know Me

We met a few years ago
quite by surprise
I opened my eyes
and there you were

Then some years passed
And a new love came
Pleasure and pain
Things didn't remain
The same

I saw you again
When I left him
You know me
I can tell
My heart recognizes
You very well

I know you'll
be waiting for me tomorrow
Because
Tonight I feel such sorrow

Feeling Lonely

"Hello"
You said with certitude
Smiling as I replied
unsuspectingly -
We talked and laughed
I liked your attitude
Inside - I was so glad
Your attention
I really had

All along
I was a game to you
Your intentions
Were not to be true
Sure - stamping on my heart
Made me blue
Mister -
Here's a news flash
For you

You had your chance
To treat me coldly
ONLY
Because I was feeling lonely
Someone will show you
How it feels
To be walked on
By the heels

On that day
The tables will turn
Your heartache
You've truly earned

Dangerous Decision

You welcomed me
into your life
with a friendly gesture

We enjoyed laughing together
conversing
and sharing meals too
Quickly - our friendship grew

Reconsideration
of a complicated situation
I was determined
that we must part

Months passed
and
Our separation didn't last
You expressed your heart
and
I want a new start

Here we are again
Making
A
DANGEROUS DECISION

Released

Spell bound by
your touch
Controlled by dreams
you promised
False feelings of security
that you will always be mine
Faded realities
gone with time
Can't hold on
Must let go
I'm released from
emotions that held you close
And now
My life continues
with your love at a distance

All for Me to Hold

If only the tenderness
of your heart
could never ever part
The security of your embrace
could be for me in any case
The comfort of your voice
could mellow my mind
for a long time
The sweetness of your lips
could pleasure mine
as often as the sunshine
The strength of your spirit
could share when I'm near it
If only the depth of your soul
could be all for me to hold

MOODS OF COMFORT

Comfort of Change

To experience the end -
Actually is to experience
a new beginning

That is the comfort of change

A Prayer

Grant me the strength
to move forward
in life -

Grant me the wisdom
to make improved
decisions

If I Had…

If I had a chance
to win romance
your gentle way
would make my day

If I had a dream
of peace and love
you would appear
with a dove

If I had one wish
to come true
most certainly
I'd wish for you

Warm Whispers of True Love

My heart wants
to surround you close
as complete as soft blue
covering the sky

My lips want
to appreciate the tenderness of yours
as sweet as the quench of a thirst

My touch wants
to embrace all of you with comfort
as my blanket of love preserves with warmth

My mind wants
to receive
as you penetrate the depths
of my soul
with your mental message

My body wants
you to know the pleasure
as smooth as the touch of soft velvet
and the silkiness of black satin

My eyes want
to seduce desire
as gentle as your warm whispers of true love

You Knew

When my eyes
didn't look into yours that day
So much that reaction
really did say

You knew
when my mind seemed far away
while we spent time together
in our usual way

You knew
when I held your hand
tighter during the game we played

You knew
when my tears fell on your shoulder
in a special way

You knew
I loved you
before I could say

When Two Souls Touch

Unknown to me before our union -
The depths of beauty
When two souls touch

Cycle of Endless Passion

This time I know it's real
I know because of how I feel

You bring pleasure to my world
day and night
Thoughts of us together
sends me in flight
You are different and make
me feel special
A cycle of endless passion
has nestled

Morning Love

Waking from
deep slumber -
Joyful and peaceful
hearts together -
Exceeding the surge
of thought
While exploring the
Wonderful high of passion
We sought
Tenderly you enter mine
as
Pleasure whispers echo -
love sensations powerful
and bold
My quivers excite
Our eyes unite
We embrace so tight
Like magic from above
So sweet is your
Morning Love

Let Me

Let me...
Pleasure you with the sensation of love
Let me...
Calm your fears
Let me...
Watch your body tremble as the splendor of high emotions surround you completely
Let me...
Comfort you and embrace you closely with the warmth of my affection

State of Innocence

Obvious excitement has swept you away
The need for physical satisfaction is desired
My voice and my caress is all you ask
As you controlled the actual feeling
I watched your pleasure
And thought - how unique this situation
After feeling complete, you submerged to a state of innocence

Rarity

Feelings
resembling none
I've known before -
Your presence in my life
has opened a new door
Your handsome style
and
Grand finesse
Brightness my days
I do confess
Always willing to give a
helping hand
I often think to myself
"Oh what a man"

Appreciating my desire to want
good love - you are close
in heart - fitting like a glove
As we discover more about our
attraction - I'll never forget
my initial reaction -
When I realized what has
happened to me - you
My friend, are a rarity

Unleashed

Your soothing way
makes my day
Your smile leaves
me wanting for awhile
Your tender touch
commands without demand
You're unleashed over
my soul
To you, I surrender my control

My Spring Time

As the new buds form
on the trees
Soon there will be
bright flowers among the
green leaves
Sweet scents of honeysuckle,
lilac and lavender
will fragrance the air
You appear -
bringing comfort to my fears
Embracing my soul
with tender rapture
My love and devotion
you have captured
All winter long -
I looked for a sign
Here you are -
my spring time

Gentle Love
A gift from you
to me
Exquisite and flowing
so gracefully
A delicate blossom
nurtured with care
So gentle is your love
and nothing can compare

Beyond

Appealing from the moment
I saw you
Desires blossom
while I'm around you
Warmth and compassion
so delicious
Cupid's arrow extended
I'm unsuspicious
Charmed by your handsome
smile
Captured by your gentle
style
Embraced by your wisdom
and grace
Amazed by your
impeccable taste
Qualities I'd hoped for
and more
You possess ranking
a perfect score
Our hearts radiate with
love's bond
Reality of us
has gone
Beyond

GUEST POEMS

I'm honored to introduce
and share
the poetic talents of
I. Wynette Millner
and Bennie Cochece Barnes

Someday
I. Wynette Milliner

Here's my heart
it's yours for the taking
It's been around for awhile
be careful of its breaking...

I've waiting for someone true
who'll love and care for me
maybe an old friend -
perhaps one that's very new

I've longed for a special someone
to wipe away my tears
We shall walk hand and hand
and share our remaining years

I wish to hold you in my arms
cradling all cares and doubts
nestled against the warmth of my caring
that's what love's about

Someday
Someday
Someday...

Courtesy with Concern
Bennie Cochece Barnes

You always seem to ask me -
Are things OK?
Is it alright? Is something else
you say

You always talk with manners
unique and very meek
A great and confident planner
with so many things to seek

You always seem to smile
even when you know it hurts
It lasts for only a while
as you deal with fast talks and flirts

I like your conversation
and the way you carry yourself
You do it with such moderation
fits like a book on a shelf

You write with such explicity
with a touch of love
It leaves their minds in a mystery
a talent from God above -

As times goes on
I'm beginning to learn
That you are filled with
courtesy, with concern

BOOK III:
OBSTACLES

1992

Dedication

Obstacles is dedicated to my uncle,
Mr. Bill Rice, and my aunt,
Mrs. Phyllis Rice, because you
are both very special sparks of
inspiration and care through
times in my life when
I need you most. I love you.

Acknowledgements

Your love and support are precious to me: Luis Torres, Jackie Coleman, Kelly McCarron, Asaki, Gwendolynne Osborne, Lecia Warner, Sandy Williams, Wendy Watson, Abdul Sulaymen, Samad Gamble, David C. Cherry, Joylette R. Branson, James Spells

Special thanks to my creator, without you I am not.

Introduction

Life is filled with never-ending events.
We all experience pleasure and pain
in levels of expectations and surprises.
Obstacles is a revelation of never
ending events of the heart.
I am pouring out raw emotion,
totally gripping, and surrounding
you with reality.

Dilemmas and intricacies reveal
our capacity to cope with
various circumstances.

I invite you to experience Obstacles as I exemplify contention and
pursue tranquility. I guarantee a new attitude.

PATHWAY TO REALITY

Finally, Reunited

Days and nights escaping -
patiently, we were waiting

We set forth to discover
how we could recover
from a long separation
of pain and aggravation

Determined to make our dreams
come true
With love, we continued to pursue

Once we found ourselves together
We knew this love was forever

Finally, Reunited As One
Our lives seemed to have just begun

You Know Me

We met a few years ago
quite by surprise
I opened my eyes
and there you were
Then some years passed
And a new love came
Pleasure and pain
Things didn't remain
The same...
I saw you again
When I left him
You know me
I can tell
My heart recognizes
You very well
I know you'll
be waiting for me tomorrow
Because
Tonight I feel such sorrow

When I first met heartache - I was surprised
Vowing to not let it come again---
It returned somehow.

Just A Phase
I shared my heart
a gamble
I took anyway
You said -
you believe me
but
it is just a phase
Time passes quickly
at the moon and stars
I gaze
I fell in love with you
You said
you believe me
but
it is just a phase
Painful moments came when
I knew I must let
you go
My tears fell on your shoulder
in such an overflow
You know how real
deep in my heart I feel
I was left dazed
but
it was just a phase

Lonely Heart

Sitting here thinking
of my past happy days
and the reasons for
the smiles back then
Every possible thought
continues to lead
towards my heart's
contentment
All the joys and realities
of life - I feel

But now

I have a lonely heart
and I don't like this deal
Soon, Someday my heart
won't feel lonely
until that time
I'm content with
good friends only

Live the Moment
I don't want
to think about tomorrow
I don't need
the pressures of consequence
I don't like
the complications
of us together
I want to live the moment
and enjoy our time as one

Difficulties
Times of happiness
and
Times of pain
We experience hardships
and
We gain
Knowledge of life and ourselves
Keeps us moving forward
To unveil
The beautiful realities
of our difficulties
Bringing us closer
to our future

Web of Love

Tangled inside my mind
Feelings in my heart
deepened with time
Caught and suspended
a thin thread
of faith
Snared with a love
that is so great
A web of love
do I escape
Tossing and turning
no answer
to be found
Surrounded, entwined
deeper
I'm bound
Control I must seek
to save my soul
This love, I must keep
this is my goal

Inside My Prison

From inside my prison
Me
Myself
and
I look out
Through bars of hope

Holding on with clenched fists
Emotions locked up
Waiting to escape
Counting days filled
with emptiness and pain

Release me
and you'll see
Love hungers for
the taste of
an accepting embrace

Understand and please
erase
my sadness and tears

Give me a place
in your heart
I can call home

Revelation of Hearts

You said ---
you felt this way
long ago

You couldn't tell me then
because of fears

I was touched
inside --- I cried
happy tears

To know the one I love
has loved me too ---
Is a revelation of hearts
beautiful
and
true

…Until the End

I want you to understand
my fears and dry
my tears

I want you to capture
the security of tender
rapture

I want you to feel
that my heart
is for real

I want you to embrace
my desires and flaming
passions

I want you to know
how much I love
you so

I want you to recall
sweet memories of
our past

I want a love that will
last and last

I want you to share
my life until
the end

I'll Wait for You

My heart is in control
Your love is my goal
To have and to hold
Forever and always
I'll wait for you ---

How Long

So long
How long?
Long ago
How long?
Until...

Deep

Look inside my soul
through my eyes
Feel the rhythm
of my heart
as we embrace
Taste the sweetness
of my love
you caress
the softness
Nurture the essence
as it flows
Deep within
your love goes

...Time Passes Anyway

Living for today
or tomorrow
I still feel
deep sorrow
...time passes anyway

Losing a precious love
that lingers in my heart
only distance keeps
us apart

Hoping and wishing
upon a star
for the emptiness to fade away
or
unite me with a new love today
...time passes anyway

Life's essence and sweetness
is gone
Silent tears continue on
...time passes anyway

Please Understand

To be in-love with someone you can't share your life
-- because of a complicated situation is a pain
in your heart that remains forever.

The following poem is dedicated
to the best love for the most reasons.

Loving you
through and through
You know how much
from the things we do
Our lives will continue
brighter than before
Our special way as one
brings comfort galore
As the months pass
dark shadows cast
upon the gleam in our eyes
Puddles of tears
clouding the way for us
to say good-by
Perhaps
Another time or another place
united again you and I
Now --- we must
adhere to the plan
Only through our love
we part
Please understand
you are close
in heart - always

Now That You Are Here

As a young girl
I smiled and flirted
with my eyes
because I was too shy
to tell my heart

As I matured
excitement ventured
into my life
I committed early
without hesitation

As I learned
more about life
and myself
my challenge to continue
proved courage

As I developed
my sensuous nature
I began to explore

Now that you are here
I want to know more

A Wish
You told me
You'll always be there
to show you care

you'll always love me
was the key
that opened my heart
and helped me see

I made all the difference
in your life
removing stress and strife

If things could change
you would embrace
only me

Once upon a time
I had a wish
For the first star
I see
In the sky
until you said good-bye

Memories of A Future Without You

Fun and laughter
while sitting
by the waterfront for hours

Surprise bouquets
of pretty flowers
with notes to say
I love you always

Times of happiness
and new plans everyday

Life was new
and beautiful
what more can I say

Memories of a future
without you
because I'm here now
where are you

MEMORIES
ALL I HAVE
ARE
MEMORIES

My Journey
Traveling life's road
as planned
With or without a man
Long term or short term stay
I'll continue my journey
anyway

How About You
Thinking
Where do we go
from here
Are the feelings
real enough to
survive the strain
Will the heart
endure the pain

Don't Do Me This Way

We talked and laid it all out
Hours past our date
you're not here
no call

Now I'm in doubt

My first hope is that you're O.K.
And then I think to myself
Please - Don't do me this way
Minutes pass and I'm
worried, scared, sad and mad
Remember the understanding we had
You said, "Give me one more time.
Baby I promise not to let you down again."
I kept my faith in your words
Was that a sin

A relationship of love, trust
compassion, understanding
Was it me -- was it something
you needed to say
Please - Don't do me this way

You know by now your absence
is hurting and tension is building
Is this the one more time
you promised ---
way back when
Baby you've done it again
My thoughts as I lay ---
Don't do me this way

PATHWAY TO TRANQUILITY

Reunion in December

Over a year has passed since I saw you last
I extended an invitation for you to join me
at a December celebration
Handsome and fine
you were on time
A nice gentle smile
with red and white roses for me
You were thoughtful and sweet
Our Reunion In December
It Is Something To Remember
The evening was ours
as we talked, danced
and gazed with pleasure
Everyone at the party could truly see
our contentment had no measure
Events that led to your warm hospitality
brought us to a new reality
Our Reunion In December
It Is Something To Remember
Special and kind
you were to me
In my heart -- thoughts of you
will always be
Especially of
Our Reunion In December
It Is Something To Remember

They Don't See...

Others may say things
to make you smile
their shallow words
last for just a little while

They want to have you alone
for a hour or two
to take but not to
really give to you

That's no way to live
left empty and never to be filled
Handsome and fine
you are indeed

Frequent invitations
you'll continue to receive
But they don't see
the beauty I see

Our conversations
pursue and explore
overtime we learn more
Your kind and gentle way revealed to me everyday
Your depths of understanding
reach beyond any measure

Your friendship ---
I'll always treasure
The essence of your being
relates to me

They don't see
the beauty I see

Much of yourself you do share
shows me how much you do care
I see the light deep inside you
wanting to shine more than it gets to

Clever with good intent
Wisdom of life assures
from Him you were sent

Special to me you truly are
No one I know can match
you by far

My words aren't meant to flatter
My expressions are appreciation
of your good character
You deserve to have your light
shine through and through

You are a bright star to me
And
They don't see
the beauty I see

Sunshine Don't Go Away

I've told you of my joy
I've whispered my strong feeling
I wasn't coy
I've showed you my heart
with pride -- expecting
no promise in return
a new lesson I've learned
I've embraced you close
while my imagination captured my desire
to have you know me deep within
I've kissed you with
tenderness and care
I've smiled at you because
I was glad you were there
I've listened to you share
your deep thoughts -- and I've gained
I've watched you absorb
my many talks of pain
I've gazed into your eyes
continuously because they warm my soul
I've wondered about my future
with you -- As If I could be so bold
I've opened my mind
to a new level of love
you are my sunshine
shining from above
I've realized I need
you close in my heart
and I don't want us to ever part
Sunshine Don't Go Away
Continue to Nurture Me Day After Day

Phase of Love

A phase of love
Accepting the presence of what is ---

Pondering the consequence
of what might be

Exploring the essence
of reality

A phase of love
that embraces patiently

You Choose Me

They are around you
always - the others
looking at you in a daze

Short, Tall, Beautiful and Fine

For them - you have
no time
Anticipating the moment
we meet
Your gentle hugs and kisses
are so sweet
Looking into your eyes
love I see
That's why
you choose me

Love Has No Plan

My thoughts travel
deep
Pondering this love
I must keep
So special
and unique
This love I didn't
seek
But here it is
in my hand
I'm holding it close
as I can
Love is love
and
Love has no plan

Exception

Never - Ever
Could I
or
Would I
Until our connection ---
You are my exception

Heart and Soul

Alluring my heart
so sweet and natural
Just as the taste of honey
treasured by the bee

Surrounding my soul
so beautiful and complete
Just as paradise and deep waters
of a tranquil sea

So Nice, So Kind, So Right

Smooth motions of pleasure
embrace me
so nice
Sweet echoes of warmth
I hear
so kind
Sensual excitement
feels
so right

Love-Making

Softly stroking
my mind
with verbal romance

Surrounding desire
with certainty

Pouring passion
freely 'til I blend
with you
and the sweet melody
of love sounds

Caressing
Sensating
Breath-taking
Love-Making

Welcome Back

My lonely heart
missed you everyday
Sadness in my eyes revealed
more than words
could say
The warmth of your
smile
is so pleasing
The thoughts of your
love
is teasing
Testing our love
has opened the door
Welcome Back
Sunshine
I need you
more
and
more

Virgin Love

Various emotions
confessed
Your heart's treasure
expressed
I now know
you care so
Through timeless
emptiness
You rescued and nurtured
like the sun up above
Tenderly -- you told me
I'm your virgin love

I Believe

I Believe
in miracles
I Believe
you love me
I Believe
together we'll find
answers in life
yes that's the key
I Believe
in your words of care
I Believe
you'll always be there
I Believe
I will make your world
complete
I Believe
in you and me

A Chance

A friendly hello
"How are you today?"
Responding with a smile
I said "O.K."

Unsuspectingly ---
You are the one
in my dreams

Bringing love
to quench and to please
Time revealed
the best of us

More and more
we began to trust

Now -- we are in love
Because at a glance
We decided to take
a chance

Just Like A Flower

Unfolding slowly
As I learn of my
inner-self
Life is my mother
teaching and nurturing
my progress
Petals extending
As my heart
to bring joy and
pleasure while you adore
Delicate existence
endures the storm
returning year after year
more magnificent than before
Vivid shades beyond
the rainbow colors
create my rare beauty
Radiating proudly
as I discover
my unique quality
My season is now
and you are my first prize
Just like a flower
I'm a blossom
in your eyes

Side by Side

As I think back
to past relations
I realize how special
you are to me

No one can compare
to our situation
Your love is given
so sweetly

Deep inside
we are as one
Growing together
nurtured by
the sun

Somewhere
Somehow
We'll live like
our dreams

You and I
Side by side
Forever like
an endless stream

Saying... I Love You

You've taken time
to know me ---
to figure me out
through and through

And still
here you are
holding me
tighter and tighter
Saying... I love you

A Blue Moon

Unique quality of love
shines inside my heart

Depth of sincerity
measured while we
were apart

I want to know
why you are different
from the rest

Night and day
I've been put
to the test

The answer will come
to me soon

Every now and then
there is a blue moon

How Deep Dare I Go

Replenish my heart
with essential love strokes

Let me drink the sweet taste
of comfort --
for I am thirsty

Avail your precious moments
to caress my high passions

Intrigue my mind
combined with security
and understanding

Embrace my wishes
and let me know

How Deep
Dare I Go

GUEST POEMS

For My Elders and Relatives
(and for those whose business it never was)
By Gwendolynne F. Osborne

You lift yourselves above humanity.
You frown upon my very being,
with distasteful contempt.

And I have come to you with innocence asking
your pardon, and your forgiveness.
I have not asked for forgiveness even without
actions that have shown my sincerity.

Now I choose to hold myself.
I choose to hold onto myself.
No longer needing to reach to you...
except that you would reach to me for
the purposes that
we might heal.

Tears, tears, so many tears after you my elders, anguished tears after you my elders refused to teach me with your support when I was younger and naive... as I fell deeper into my inexperience and you gazed and murmured and complained about my life. I thought I was bad and deserving of pain and you were even happy about it.

But Now... I choose to pick up my life and be gone away from your cruelty. I lift my thoughts above your thoughts of who I am or am not. I am now free to see my beauty, free to validate my life, free to seek my purpose for being now.

I am free to be happy. For I, like you, am Mother and Father Goddess' child.

The Recipe for Life
By Samad Gamble

Man and woman - a perfect start
They give life - then fall apart
What they need is:
A tablespoon of self-esteem
and a dream

A teaspoon of trust
not just lust
A cup of real love
from up above

Two cups of self owed peace
the peace must increase
Two cups of understanding
for the hard landing

Stir and mix well, the Recipe For Life
couldn't be cut with the sharpest knife -
for this is the key
and the Recipe For Life

It is my pleasure to introduce the poetic talents of Ms. Miriam Ortiz. Miriam, your beautiful expressions compares to your beautiful spirit - thank you for sharing with us.

Thief

I loved you purely; you stole from me
I loved you genuinely; couldn't you see

You let me go on believing it was true
I needed to trust; what else could I do

One year of my life, you had me believe
You loved me dearly, yet now you retrieve

I want my heart back - erase my pain
You stole from me - you have no shame

Doing Time

Lack of love have not I for my friends
are all there
Yet alone I stand with this empty
lonely stare
I feel incomplete - my puzzle undone
Oh God up above
When will I find the special one
What have I done
To get this affliction
the pain of loneliness
Has no conviction
Why do I write
No one will hear my cry
Lord in the heavens
Please tell me why
What's wrong with me
I don't understand
Why am I alone
In this vast spacious land
It feels - I shall never have someone
To be mine
Imprisoned am I
Behind Bars
Doing Time

I Apologize

Who Am I
to right a wrong
The days of special
are long gone
I closed the entrance
to the bliss I sought
The low down dirty blues
is all I caught
A new day
has come again
This time I won't pretend
Today I remove
my disguise
To myself - I apologize

BOOK IV:
APPROACH...
IF YOU DARE

1995

Dedication

This section of this book is dedicated to my beautiful grandmother, Mrs. Elsie Fortune.

Grandmom you have inspired my continuum and encouraged me to live my dreams - I love you and I am very proud of our journey together.

From My Heart and Soul,
Norahs

Special Thanks To...

- My Creator, for my poetic gift and for sustaining my existence.
- My Ancestors, for your guiding spirits.
- Mr. Irving DeShields, for being the man you are and contributing to my growth.
- Ms. Pauline Williams, for listening and supporting me with a cheerful smile.
- Ms. Charlene Smith, for always being honest, I like your style my friend.
- Mrs. Esther HamzidKhan, for your mother-love and wit.
- Mr. Larry Jones, for keeping me smiling with Snoopy, Garfield, and your heart!
- Mr. Martino Mason for sharing your love, high spirited personality and keeping faith.
- My Parents, Rayful and Elouise for your patience and understanding as I seek my universal purpose and inner peace.
- Thanks Dad for the title "Approach"
- My Guest Poets, Ms. Gwendolyne F. Osborne, Mr. Warren Oree and Ms. Miriam Ortiz - thanks for your poetic contributions to "Approach... If You Dare" and supporting my quest.
- My endless list of artists, friends and supporters who nurture my courage and strength.

    I love you All,
    Norahs

Introduction

The art of life is how you execute the choices you make. By design, I choose "Approach... If You Dare" to highlight and encourage my continuum. My direction is forward and "Approach... If You Dare" has an attitude of conquest. My strategy is faith and circumstance will present each challenge.

My technique is "just do it" because talking about it delays results. My method is "life" because this gift I must not for take for granted, and clarity is reality.

"Approach... If You Dare" is my testimony of will and sweet harmony before my summit. I am on a journey that clings to faith for endurance. I am accomplishing and overcoming the impossible dream, while simultaneously healing my soul.

Ultimately, the essence of my spirit embraces peace.

MY DIRECTION IS FORWARD...

Now I'm Ready

You reached a level of love
before
I could see
I was taking my time
exploring life
just being me
Closer to you
my heart was attracted
more and more
my passion and love
reacted
Being together is what
I want for us
Understanding, guidance
and most of all trust
You hesitate when I tell you
how much I care
My desire for you is deep
and you are so rare
Accept my loving heart
that continues to beat steady
In your life is where
I want to be
and
Now
I'm ready -

Quiet Ocean

When you look
Absorb my vast-endless existence
as I engage purity and universal will
to express my calm and fury
When you embrace
Touch my liberated spirit of tranquility
that journey's on a path
of faith and appreciation
When you remember
Feel the pleasure and excitement
of a rainbow reflecting prisms
of joyful desires
When you listen
Fear not the echoes of my pain
as I emerge from past hurt
Then pour your horizon of radiant
beauty and love to gently kiss
my quiet ocean -

Freedom to Love

The desires and passions I have
for you are as natural as the...
green leaves with a tiara of spring dew
as natural as the...
clear morning air filled with early birds
joyful songs
as natural as the...
sweet coolness in the breeze before
the sun's rays warms with calm
as natural as the...
steady rhythm of my heart beat
filled with appreciation and reprieve
as natural as the...
delicate pattern of waves motioning
the seas
as natural as the...
dancing snowflakes on a crisp winter evening
as natural as...
my rolling tears when I feel you leaving
as natural as the...
discovery that we are meant to be you and I
as natural as the...
freedom to love and be loved
before I die

My Innocent Desire

Charismatic attraction
stimulates
Magnetizing reaction
penetrates
Through layers of lingering emotions
from before
My innocent desire
opens a new door
Embraced by feelings _ I thought
were gone forever
Quench my thirst for the sweetness
as we entwine together
Pouring raw passion into the
gold chalice of wonder
We drink the nectar as one
to discover
My innocent desire
is like no other -

STRATEGY IS FAITH

Comfort Cove

A cascade of moments
filled with excitement
A drizzle of wishes
come true
A splash of soft whispers
to entice my intrigue.
A shower of sweet smiles
brings girlish blush
to my cheeks
A tide of tender affection
calms and soothes
I tremble with anticipation
as we blend and groove
Pouring passion here and there
our comfort cover
is crystal clear

This Place I Call Home

This is the place I call home
because I feel
comfortable and cozy
because I see
my fantasies become realities
because I hear
the welcoming echo of love
because I smell
the sweet aroma of contentment
because I taste
the wonderful blessings
from GOD above
because when I'm here
I'm not alone
This is the place I call home

Ashanti Goddess
(Inspired by the musical tune by Byard Lancaster)

Imagine the taste of sweet pleasure
pure nectar of love to treasure
Gentle now - you must handle with care
Give, receive and it's all there
a touch of wonder
she is special and unique
A queen, a goddess of love to seek
ASHANTI, ASHANTI, ASHANTI, ASHANTI, ASHANTI

A Safe Place
Where few discover
deep down inside
Where there is an aroma
of courage
Where strength is stored
for the battle of peace
Where beautiful memories
of special times gone past
Where my destination
is in reach
Where it is just me and I
to converse
Where my spiritual existence
Springs eternal

Mr. Warren Oree of Arpeggio Jazz Ensemble
has many talents to treasure and cherish.
I am honored to debut his poem "What Is It?"
Thank you Mr. Oree for sharing with us.

What Is It?

Sometimes my love
Just drips out and runs all over the place
Like some faucet that's broke,
Can't turn it off no matter how hard I try
Turn too hard and it'll break and run forever
Getting everybody wet

Sometimes, my love
Won't take no for an answer
Like some stubborn mule
Won't budge from what it wants for nobody
Push too hard and it'll lift its hind legs
And kick whoever gets too close to it
Sometimes, my love
Just won't be still
It zips about like some angry bee
Going in all directions... bumping and bouncing off
Whoever gets in its way
And if you try to stop it
It'll sting whoever it lands on

Sometimes my love
Shouts and screams all night long
Keeping everybody awake

It won't be quiet for one minute
And if you tell it to stop screaming
It stands up and shouts
for the whole world to hear

Sometimes my love
Ain't like love at all
It's more like a bully
Who want its way
No matter who gets hurt
Is that love?
If it is
I don't want nobody
To love me like that

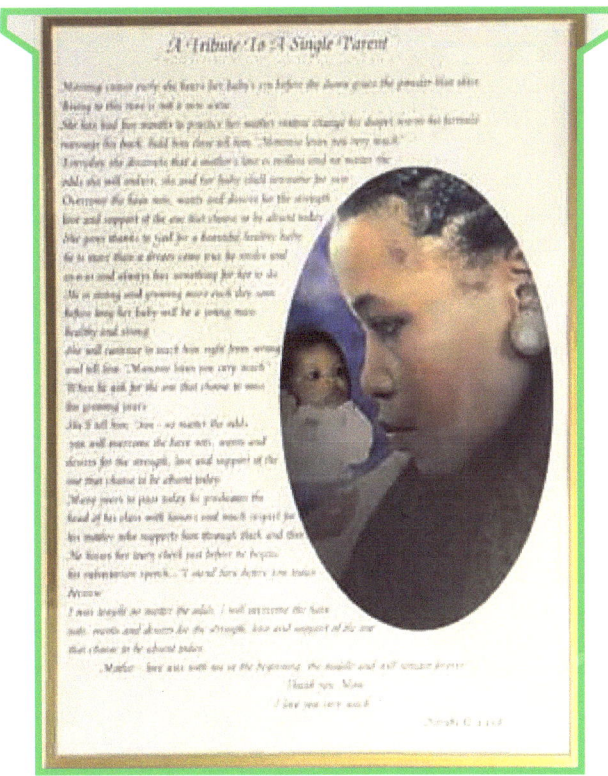

Sometimes…
The summer rain
leaves a sweetness in the
warm breeze

Sometimes…
the deep velvet sky
comforts the chill at night

Sometimes…
the single yellow rose
says more than a dozen

Sometimes the smile in your
eyes erases my doubts

Sometimes the quiet
and your presence is
enough

But this time
It's your soul that
humbles my love

One Day With You

Our first half hour
you'll read poetry to me
Bring a feeling of ease
and comfort complete
Our day continues in a place
reserved for you and I
Cozy and quaint under God's sky
smiles and laughter
reveals most of the story
We find in our souls
HER HOLY GLORY
To understand why you are here
for me
One day with you
bring life to my fantasy

Nectar of Love

Quiver my mind
with tenderness and romance
Calm my passion
with a tranquil flow
Repress with courage
my frenzy emotions
Seduce with charm
my smile of joy
Embrace my touch me and
Quench with my nectar
of Love

TECHNIQUE IS JUST DO IT

Ginger Brown

Wanting hands saturated
with coco butter scented lotion
As he watched and anticipated
the slippery feel when he
caressed my ginger brown curves
Salivating desire blended
deeply and certainly
I knew the best was
yet to come

AROMA OF PASSION
(A Short Story)

An aroma of passion intoxicated the air. I never thought he would be there - among the glistening gowns and tuxedos all around.

There he was smiling with his handsome style. Immediately, I glanced to my left for a mirror check. Then, I proceeded in his direction - leaving just enough distance for his peripheral vision to capture my image... just enough distance for his senses to be enticed by my seductive scent that many rave about.

My heart's rhythm increased as I lead a scented trail to the balcony for him to follow. I attempted to open the French Doors when a warmth gently embraced my hand and a tender whisper echoed, "May I" - I responded, "Yes, thank you, " with a captivated smile.

We entered the balcony and I felt his visual touch magnetize my desire for untamed pleasure. He asked with anticipation, "What is that fragrance you are wearing?" I smiled an I've-got-a-secret-smile and slowly leaned closer to him, just enough to ignite passion as I felt his breathing inside the smooth curve of my neck. Our fingers searched and embraced as the moistness in the center of our palms bonded our touch. My wanting lips slowly parted and his wanting lips slowly parted and we both said YES.

YOU KNOW THE TYPE
(A Short Story)

He was suave, debonair, so fine, on time - shows up at night, you know the type. No doubt about our attraction. My penetrating eyes rolled over a physique of muscle after a mental love making session that aroused the fantasy taboo of loving a stranger. I thought of why now and why not - so long as protection came first.

His well rehearsed words and actions were a woven blanket of certainty that surrounded my vulnerable emotion - let this be true. Long term plans uttered and tangible tidbits left here and there on occasional visits. I thought he must be for real -

But I'll remain a little cautious - my verbal probe of his mental vibration waved a few red flags. I'll have to hold back my lusty desires a little longer while I question his motives and my own.

Several calls to the phone number he rendered so easily started to shadow doubts and he was never there. His calls to me became less frequent. He never called or showed up for the date he planned.

The stages of disappointment, disenchantment, disbelief monopolized my mind. I questioned my judgment, I felt foolish. Once again, emptiness filled my heart. How do I erase this pain?

Erase the Pain

The sun sets and rises
some days bring new
surprises -
Swept away by
joy and pleasure
a man of good taste
beyond standard measure
Lavish my mind
with style and respect
My shielded heart is fragile
I must protect
A few days - treated like a queen
because I'm deserving
you know what I mean
There is much to gain
while allowing someone else
to erase the pain

Stroke of Love

So cool - smooth and
suave
That's how I see you
All the time
Can you ever
Do you ever
Get wild
That's the mystery
about you-um-m
I sigh
Don't pass me
by - I want you
to see in my eyes
the desire to know
your soul - to feel
your stroke of love
as I lose control
to hear the whispers
of joy and pleasure
to taste the splendor
of a fantasy come true
to know the embrace
of me and you
Surrender your beast
and let me see
How intimate we can be

It Must Be Fate

Hot and cold
sweaty and wet
These are the feelings
I continue to get
When you appear before my eyes
Although I've tried
I can't disguise
What is it about you
I question with grace
Is it your face
that do me this way
Is it your smile
or your friendly style
Is it your sexy way
that makes my day
Is it all of the above
that embraces me so
Perhaps it is your eyes
that won't let go
Whatever it is - this feeling is great
Whatever it is
It must be fate

Until You…
I didn't have the courage
to strut and sway
or shake it and make it that way

I would never have taken
or received
given or believed
I could feel so relieved

I no longer have to imagine
how special it would be
between you and me

I shouldn't want even more
after our wet and wild magic
performs - but I do

I couldn't have known of the
tasty thrill and seductive sizzle
between two -
until you

Chosen Lover

Special places, expensive dinners
Crystal on ice
Bright lights, fancy cars and limousines
U-m-m-m sounds kinda nice

They ravish me with fox, mink and pearls
tantalizing bait to catch a material girl
Oh-h but that's not the way
to rock my world

Impress me, test me
Call it what you will
Been there, Did that
No fun, no thrill

I want the one that
smiles from within-
He's gentle, polite
and never offends
He's fine, exciting and
Keeps me aware
That with only him
do I dare -
Just as time recycles the sun
He's my chosen lover
He's a son-of-a-gun
He has a style of his own
Peaceful, Respectful
Suave and Debonair
With flowing waves

In his fresh-cut
Dark brown hair
Picture milk chocolate and oh so sweet
he tenderly melts
In our tender night heat

Dripping his honey love
Over and Under
His passion flower
We can just kick it
for hours and hours

He's more than a good feeling
more than a tease
He's my chosen lover
and he can certainly please
He's not too much
but just enough
He's got it going on and on
and oh yeah I like his sexy stuff

He's more than food
more than drink
He nurtures and replenishes
as I speak
His voice tickles my heart
like a magic wand
my rush is euphoric
and his call
is always on time
My desire continues to
beckon and call

Even as I sleep
I see us in the mirror
on the wall
His surprises are from
his kind heart
I blush like a young girl
around him
from the very start
he's all these things
to me and more
He's my chosen lover
the one I adore
Only those who know
really know what I feel
When a woman makes her choice
temptation has no voice
And my chosen lover
chooses me too

Breathless Anticipation

It's like that something so pretty and sweet
to lick, nibble and suck,
like a Dutch chocolate treat -

It's like a place where the depths of emotions
can drench your mind
An existence of pure pleasure
to treasure throughout time -

It's like a might love
that holds mysteries and answers
that the wise men seek
like an open secret that your
humble heart can't keep -

It's like the "should I"
and the shouldn't that says "no"
but you do it anyway -
like trust beyond the limits
of your moral fibers
because it feels good today -

It's like the smooth groove
on the radio that takes
you to a place of joy
like gripping on the hop
of getting a brand new toy -

It's like emerging from
a powerless attraction
you try to deny until
you recognize
it's the apple of your eye -

It's like the warmth of a touch
that radiates its magic
and erases the chill
like perfect passion that
controls a tender thrill

It's like the comforting oasis
in a thirsty desert of desire
like pouring your cool midnight
lust into my dreams
taking me higher and higher -

It's like any time, any place
could be right
because of the kinky wild love
you made last night -

It's like the sure real deal
that doubles your bet
and your return is more
then you imagined you would get

It's like passing a course
that's test-less
you know the overwhelming facts
leave you breathless

It's like wanting to say "yes",
if only the question could be asked
It's an insatiable appetite
It's anticipation that lasts and lasts

METHOD IS LIFE
A Good Spiritual Friend
(Message About A Friend 12/23/94)

A good spiritual friend and I were conversing on the phone last evening about our trials and tribulations in life. The flow of positive energy between us generated excitement and guidance - just what we needed at that point. One of the highlights of our conversation was making plans to be a part of the delegation from Philadelphia to Beijing, China for the Fourth Women's World Conference. This Conference is filled with many opportunities for women that we both want to experience. As our talk progressed my friend invited me to a celebration for one of her friends I hadn't met as of yet. She called the event "A Celebration of Feminine Energy" and we both liked the title so much that we decided to write about it. I find it most interested when me and my good spiritual friend are talking whether it is on the phone or in person - I'm always lifted to a higher plane of understanding and direction. I just want to publicly say

Thank you Ms. Gwen Osborne for all that you bring to my life. When we meet it is always a Celebration of Feminine Energy.

May you never be thirsty or hungry.

Peace

With respect and honor, I am pleased to present to you the poetic talents of my spiritual sister and beautiful friend Ms. Gwendolyn F. Osborne

Baton

Raised us up
beat our butts
But you passed not the baton

Slips with lace
Vaseline on our faces
But you passed not the baton

Me to the hall
then to the Church
Thanksgiving turkey
Friday night perch
But you passed not the baton

Fixed our hair to our style
We children were so young
Loved each other for a long while
Still you didn't pass that baton

You didn't pass the mother wit
or nurture us from knowledge's tit
you refused to talk to us of your pain
and we never saw you cry
Some of our souls began to wither and fold
and some of us just died

But now we've got the baton
We made it for ourselves
We got on track
We got on course
We opened to Our Spirit's Source
Through 12 steps, self helps
we spared no costs or lengths
And then a new power surged
compelling us to new and
Boundless strengths

Now we are running
to the next line
Not breaking our strides
to pass the baton
To our children's lives
so that they may take
their rightful place
In what became a huddled unfair race

In victory's tears
they will stand with life's Olympic God
in their hands
And in their hearts
They will hold their much deserved Baton

Another artistic masterpiece by
Ms. Gwendolyn F. Osborne

Untitled

I am so full of tears
Tears that will heal
My frozenness to once again feel
softly alive and warm
Streams of tears gently flowing
Full of sunlight rippled dances

A message expressed in a moment of
rage and confusion in search of healing
and understanding - embraced by freedom.
Dedicated to the conflicting mother/daughter relationships.

Dear Mother

I've learned from you
to wash clothes and
keep my home clean
To present myself well
in public with pride
Although you laughed
and made fun of
my physical make up
Your conflicting messages
laid a foundation for
much confusion and
very little understanding
of my self-worth
But that mass confusion
is the very motive for
my quest for the truth
and direction to my
universal purpose
I've discovered that
I have a reasons for living
A reason to teach
my child about
the journey
I give thanks to

my ancestors...
to the hearts and
souls that guide
my continuum -
You may never ever
acknowledge that
you are paralyzed by
deception
I'm liberated from
that shackle and
I am thankful for
the love from my
Creator

Before Love

I was adrift on the buoyant unknown
until the liberation of the shackle
that surrounded my virgin heart
NOW I HAVE FAITH
I was barefoot walking the shore of burning hot sands
until I felt the cool comforting wave
as the flow rushed around my ankles
NOW I APPRECIATE UNITY
I was nature's only blossom without a name
until you came
NOW THEY WANT ME BY THE DOZENS
I was stillness in silence
until movement
NOW I'M WIND AND I HAVE MANY SHADES OF VOICE
I was tart with bitter confusion
until the sweet nurture of love
touched my core
NOW I RADIATE UNDERSTANDING
I was tomorrow that never came
until today I realized I was yesterday
NOW I'M FOREVER PRESENT
I was a wish without a star to be upon
until I came true
NOW I LIVE MY DREAMS
I was rhythm without lyrics
until I became a song
NOW I AM A COMPOSER
I was morning without a sunrise
until my horizon became a reflection of my life
NOW I HAVE LOVE

Saturday Morning Symphony

I lay soothed by the
pleasant moist breeze
seeping through the mesh window screen

Blended echoes of the perched early birds'
chirping tempo
the roar of an airplane's engine above
and me-ows-s-s below
As I watch my cream color shears
dance with the incoming flow

The smooth jazz vibrations on my radio
add-s-s-s
to the gentle seduction
The pattern on the wall fan is exotic
and I escape to an enchanted place of pleasure

Closer I'm magnetized to explore his enticing neck
and shoulders with my tender kisses
a routine morning greeting with added charm

My hands travel with wanting caress
My breathing harmonizing with
the early bird's orchestra
My senses massaged with rhythmic desire

A Saturday Morning Symphony
lifting me higher
and
higher

This Could Be You

At the bus stop, on church steps,
in the subway halls
With children, mobile beds,
blankets, bags of clothes and all
What was -- What is
the plight for this fall
How can we - how would we
make it dissolve
I have a thought - I have a plan
look inside my heart to understand
They are people - like you and I
with a beginning - a middle
at the end we all will die
Today is the day I must make a change
if only with one other
then we've gained
Two steps towards progress
the effort is in motion
Unity is more than just a notion
On the other foot
fits the shoe
Now -- do you have a clue
THIS COULD BE YOU --

Butterfly
A vision of beauty
bright and free
Spirited with celebration
and harmony
Blossoms of peace
and faith
Extensions of elegance
and grace
Rainbow of wisdom
and content
More than a pot of gold
I've been sent
Reality has touched my essence - I
can't deny
Radiance in flight
like a butterfly

Reminiscing the Joys of You

How you held me close and calmed my stormy mood
How you always knew when and understood
How you taught me about laughing, just kicking it, enjoying love,
and kissing
How we watched the silent sunset as we strolled barefoot on the
wet sandy beach
hand in hand
How you smiled when I brought you breakfast
as you adjusted to a new day's light in bed
How we fantasized our love making before we made our tender
love
our sunshine
How we danced to the tune of the early birds songs - so gentle and
kind
How we captured each other inside the sky of infinite discovery
How we defined our oneness with the depths of our souls because
words left mystery
How our paradise flourished through
the rains of despair
How the flower of our passion
pollinated by the nature's design and care
how beautiful I feel and so new
reminiscing the joys of you

Kelly Drive

Dusk has merged
with day
A hazy cast
entwine the skies
More than a million
gleaming gentle waves
motion the Schuylkill
reflects in my eyes
A shadow of lavender
and melon hints its
presence without disguise
My journey on Kelly Drive
puts mellow on my mind

Certain Love

You are
the touch of comfort
my soul needs
You are
the nourishment in the
sun rays that bring life
everlasting to a seed
You are
the gentle in a breeze
that cools my flaming demand
You are
the miracle that performs
while holding my hand
You are
the tickle in the whisper
so close the echo lingers
You are
the motion that surrounds
my body when I tingle
You are
the for
in my ever- that means
so much more
You are the "o" in my ou-u-u
as I adore
You are
my innocence caressing
the softness of a gifted rose
You are
the beauty in the mirror
reflecting my image but poised with your certain love...

A King of Love

If I were God
You would be my first creation
Your smooth deep brown skin
an absolute relation
Your hair so becoming
outlining your sensuous mouth
Your enduring shoulders
will bear my burden of pain
without a doubt
Your arms assembled with
strength and grace -
hands so bold to gently
hold my face
Your body's opulence so grand
and commanding
Your intellect exudes
sensitivity and understanding
If I were God
I would make you
for me - A King of Love
and nobility

Your Tender Kiss

Amber and Crimson
Lavender and Melon
Peach and Cream
Rose and Teal
These are the colors
of my rainbow of passion
These are the colors of my dawn of bliss
These are the colors
of my stars from
your tender kiss

Celebration of Life
A Prayer

As the sun rise high
the warmth and beauty
embrace our lives
As the moon glows in a
velvet sky we need not ask why
As the cycle of life evolves
each and every day
So precious are the moments
we take time to say

BLESS IT BE MY LORD
Thank you for all you have given
Love in my heart to share with my family and friends
Hope in my life to understand when confusion is amiss
Peace in my soul to enfold revelation with content

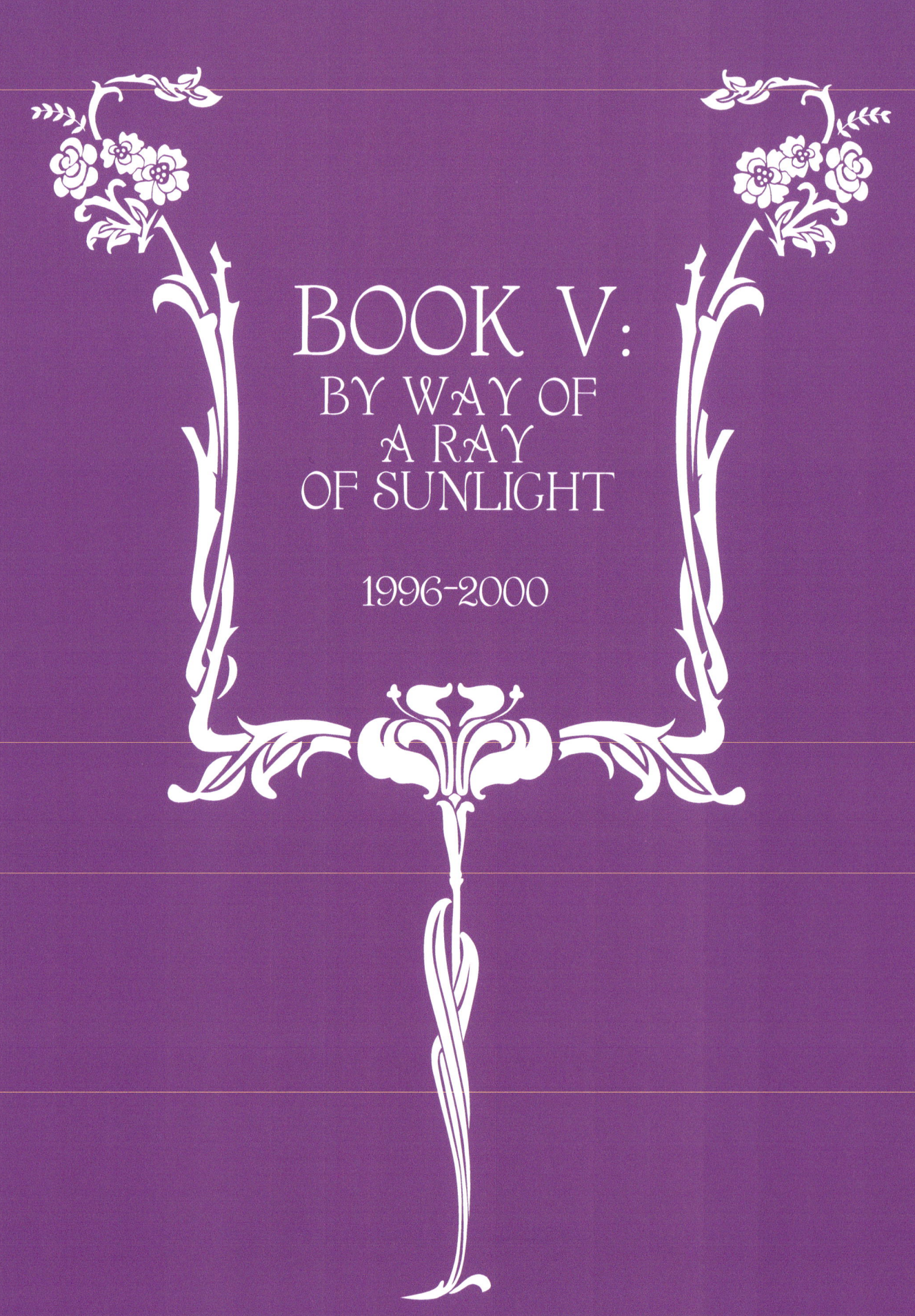

BOOK V:
BY WAY OF A RAY OF SUNLIGHT

1996–2000

Acknowledgements

All praises to my Creator for my gifts and purpose as I journey my path in life... without you I am not

Special thanks to Divine Mother-Earth for nourishment.

Respect and Honor to my ancestors that light my continuum.

Mr. Wayne Zukin, thank you for your patience and understanding and a roof over my head.

"d." aka Adjoa, thank you for your motivation, sharing your kind spirit and the computer.

Michael Pinckney, thank you for your vision and support.

Michale Lumpkin, my first cousin, thank you for your encouragement and a dream come true in Japan. I cherish the memories.

Abdul Sulaymen, thank you for your beautiful and creative photography and many words of wisdom.

My Guest Poets, thank you for making this project complete. Your talent is a treasure.

My growing list of supporters, thank you for replenishing my efforts.

I HONOR YOU ALL

Introduction

Some people keep strong by believing in nothing and some people are strong by believing in something. "By Way of A Ray of Sunshine" documents the journey traveled inside my soul... although my journey involves many pathways of truth and revered revelation, my strength and guidance is purposely protected and directed by faith.

My spiritual growth intrigues non-believers and inspires those of other convictions. You will witness peaks of eloquence, excitement and ecstasy in "By Way of A Ray Of Sunshine". You will absorb strength, courage, and find a source of enjoyment on heart-warming levels. You will be consciously elevated.

Seduction by faith captivates and blossoms externally and internally... "By Way of A Ray of Sunlight" will nurture your inner desire and you will taste the bitter-sweet nectar of experience.

Peace and Light

RED FOR PASSION WHITE FOR TRUTH...

You Are Here...
Emotions rising higher
and higher
Soft sexy rhythms traveling
entering my soul
dancing a slow sultry tango
with my spirit
Hot... Moist... Dripping...
tears of pure joy
rolling down my cheeks
as your hypnotizing voice caresses
my release of love
You absorb me and know my familiar existence
un-harness my trust... hold my heart with respect
be my eyes down this pathway to heaven
I'm blind... but confident... you are here -

There Will Never Be Another Now

I remember the day
we explored the possibilities
of us being a reality
We embraced the tender
splendor of a moment
without fear
Tasting your sweet touch
upon my lips
I savor the harmony
Open to the wisdom of a
dream come true
I kissed your vision of
pleasure and then I knew
As your whispers float deep into
my listening canal… a treasured sound
You uttered "there will never be another now"

Eclipse

Our blended existence
in the rare essence
of a time cycle

Entwined souls of a superior beauty
reflective of
the hue of absolute joy

Piercing light of truth
embraced by a blanket of eternity

Fused reality
energy that radiates exquisite love
capable of blinding
the naked heart

So Close

I was warm liquid
poured down your back
Slowly I molded into
your masculine curves
and cradled your warmth
that embraced me with tenderness
For my pleasure I caressed your spirit of peace
and I became familiar with happiness

Auras merged and journeyed
from dawn to dusk
as repetitiously as eternal bliss
Every new horizon welcomed by
your seductive kiss
Playful mornings engaged our souls
with déjà-vu
Together... once again...
So close...
Me and you

You…

You bathe me
like the energy of warm sun rays
glistening upon
my smooth chocolate brown skin
I anxiously anticipate
your return after the summer rain

You are my unpredictable mood
like the cool snowfall
in the middle of May
I was surely surprised by your visit
and I smiled as we played all day

You are my garden of precious, rare and exotic
nature's remedy to render a smile
even when I feel neurotic

You are generous portions
of good and plenty, never ending
rivers, oceans and seas of intrigue…
I am your shore of burning hot sand
your waves rush and cool without demand

You are my tears
that slowly puddle in the wells of my eyes
as we entwine and plunge deeper
in the discovery of our joy
I quiver inside your tender embrace
until your grip tightens around my waist
My passionate tears fall down my cheeks
when we lay still and our lips meet

You are my dreams
I labeled impossible
until true revelation deemed life is what
you choose it to be

You are my journey
like a pathway to moments
of inspiration, fears and triumphs
sometimes reluctant I persevere
and see the light of a new rainbow

You are my calm
in the frenzy
just being you as you are
makes me as I am
and that is a good thing we share~

Imagine…
HOT wetness rolling slowly
downward until
it meets a crevice
and decides to puddle there
There where the other hot wetness
proceeded downward into a fold
there in between… there where now it is
MOISTENED… SOAKED… DRENCHED
if you can… Imagine… how sweet
it will be when your exposed hot wetness
sizzles to the touch of my hot wetness
and together our moistened… soaked… drenched
folds form a larger puddle as our hot wet rhythms
excite velocity unknown
Our panting and deep breathing
harmonized a tempo called pure pleasure
Our spirits discovered
answers to age old questions we treasured
Can you… Yes you can
Will I… Yes I will
When? Now!
If you can… Imagine
what I've described
then together we are…
Can you imagine… ummm

I Color It Love…

When I watch a slow sunset
in the glow of a darken sky…
My vision engages warmth and calm
like you and I
I am humbled
I color it deep

When I hear the chirp of the early birds
in the dawn of the day
playful and dancing on air
my thoughts are entwined
like our special time
when we show our care
I am free
I color it choice

When I touch the soft petals
of beautiful blossoms
in the noon hour
My gift of flowers from you
is received with a smile
like the first moment
you revealed your romantic style
I am caressed
I color it gentle

When I taste the delicious nectar
of purity in a pleasure paradise
of rapture
My fantasy has given birth
to reality

I need you to cuddle me
like a newborn's mother
I am energy
I color it blessings

When I breathe in your majestic boldness
closer than close
I marinate my thoughts in a supple wind
and expand my wings to fly
I am a graceful butterfly
I color it rarity

When I think of you... us...
everything we are
I am a Goddess below and above
I color it love~

Soul to Soul

I looked inside my soul
a place where thoughts
of you dwell
I saw your smile
a ray of sunshine
I know so well
I heard your voice somewhat distant
yet near enough to stir my imagination
I felt your touch… warming and exciting
my desire and determination
I kissed your tender lips
that invite me closer
when I try to be so strong
I wanted to sing you a love song
about the joy and sadness
I sometimes feel
when you are gone
I watched you there
lingering inside my soul
your eyes reflecting the message
you dare not speak of
Because you are not yet that bold
I enjoy the feeling
when you notice my heart's rhythm
increase while you are near
I wonder why from time to time
what is your fear
You said I've been there
at least once in my life
Are you afraid that
you and I could make it twice

We can utter the most
clever words to cover up
and deny
But...
Our hearts know the truth
and our souls
know why~

LOVE MEANS LEARNING TO LET GO...

Exhale the Wait

Remember when we made our special sounds
joy sounds, happy sounds
We wined, dined and
entwined
Our world was tender... pure splendor
sweet surrender
Remember the embrace that held on forever
and a day
the pretty new sheets I put on the bed
the candle lit evenings
bubble baths for two
smooth grooves for me and you
the breakfast we ate
even though for work we were late
Remember the mental messages
that set free the inhibitions
we threw caution to the wind...
can I get a witness...
Oh yeah, how 'bout the hot buttered
honey dipped French rolls you liked so much
and the chilled sweet strawberries by the bunch
How do I say goodbye to the twinkle
in your eye... the anticipation of our rendezvous
our passion shared
We can't be through

How can you tell me now,
"Baby I really do want you"
After to another you said, "I do"?
Can you take our precious gift
to each other and reduce it
remove it
lose it
You've made your choice
I will learn to accept
and respect your decision
I will let go... to get further
I must exhale the wait~

Hostage to Guilt
The issue was
my heart
I was out on a limb
from the start
All that had been
discussed
Now is the center
of mistrust
How did we get here
to this place
known as fear
I must leave
to get a grip
I miss you
by my hip
Most of the time
I sit and wonder
with my head in a tilt
I
am
a
hostage
to guilt~

Joy In My Past

The joy of accepting you into my life
brought my heart security
happiness and less strife
I smiled pretty and
I anticipated calls from you
I was always excited when I knew
I would see you too
The time we spent
was beautiful and filled with
flowing expressions
of passion and desire
Welcoming each horizon and sunset
In your arms was the reason for my fire
Your smile held the sunshine
that glistened upon my tranquil sea
Your eyes discovered my mystery
and rendered my victory
Your laugh sang the love songs
of long ago about you and me
Your mental touch unlocked my heart
with a special key
Soon the frequency changed
your schedule was busy
and things weren't the same
The games we played
weren't special and cute
I would find myself alone
most of the time feeling aloof
Just missing you all day long
wanting to caress you come nightfall
Although changes occurred
in our lives
Without you I wouldn't have known
the splendor in the grass
Without you there would be no

joy in my past~

EVOLUTION OF A WOMAN...

Turn Around... See the Perfection

Appreciate the beauty of nature
in its purest form
in its process or progress of growth
change and discovery

Turn around... see the perfection

You are looking, seeking over anticipating
that the natural existence can be improved
by well intended disruption

It is and was there just as
it should be
by nature's design and care
Hold it and absorb in vision
Touch it with your understanding
Let your soul drink the purest juice
of God's love
It's sweet and sour pleasure enlightens
your senses~

*Conversation with Abdul on the
8th day of October 1996.
Thank you for sharing your wisdom.*

It's Your Move

Last time I was here
you were too
I was sitting just a
few rows from you
I noticed your smooth
double-dipped ebony skin
I thought to myself
here I go again
Your bright eyed gleam
over looked me
or so it seemed
Your seductive full lips
invited me in my day dream
Obvious... I was
I wondered could you see
Do you know
You are the one for me
My answer is waiting
for your question
Let's groove
The game has started
and
It's your move~

Unfinished Business

My soul yearned your presence
for many years
Thirsty for the taste of tender joy
to quench and release my fears
Set them free
to float away with ease and calm
before I could remember their existence
now they are gone
You are that familiar presence
I knew but now I meet you again
In a place far from common comfort
I have no need to pretend
We embrace the cool flame of contentment
ride the wave of dreams come true
"Time is precious"... I said to you
Stay on your mission
and I will too
Together in heart forever
we've been
Unfinished business remains
until
We are together again~

Second Choice

Brothers... Brothers... Brothers
It seems to be an ongoing fantasy
you wish to fulfill
To have a beautiful woman of body and soul
to hold you, love...
and bring you thrills
She must possess that fine
quality of seduction
She must possess that intrigue
of sensuous love and affection
She must keep you close to only her
and never stray
She must understand your wants, needs, desires
and your tender way
She must know that someday soon
is a promise but more like hope
She starts to recognize your undercover smiles
and jaded gifts are like dope
that camouflage and cloud
her reality to cope
She loses her self-respect
and direction
She plays hide and seek
ducking and dodging
her true spirit and connection
She nurtures only you and forgets that
she has a voice
No... Brother... No
I choose not to be your second choice
Take a look at yourself
deep within

Rid yourself of the naughty
that urges you to offend
This message is to those
who can relate
to help build us and make strong the weak
for goodness sake
Put universal order in your life
It starts at home with you
your mate or your wife
The responsibility is for us all to bear
No!! Brother... No!!...
Your life I cannot share
I do have a voice
I choose not to be your second choice~

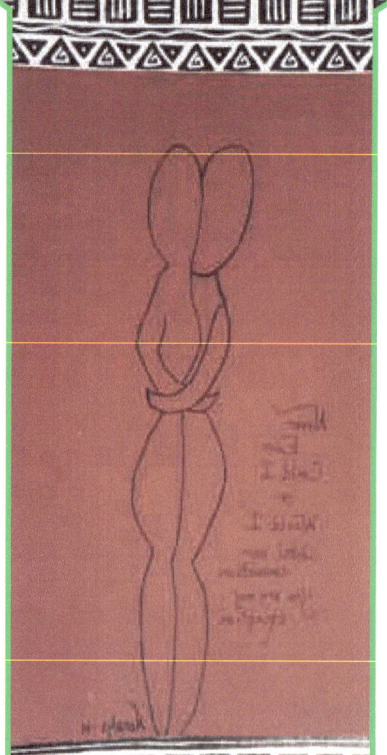

My Rite of Passage

I respect myself and others with the grace
of Rosa Parks
Gain insight and cultural awareness as I seek
and discover like beautiful Susan Taylor
Learn the truth of my heritage and speak with pride
like Beatrice Berry or Sistah Soulja when necessary
I am the extension of love and I share like my poetic mentors
Maya Angelou and Sonya Sanchez
I am blended into one walking my path of life with my head held
high
My family has set examples from which I cherish the memories
and move towards the vast sky
For who I am and who I'll become, I'm proud of my strength
as my victory is won
My ancestors light the path I follow
and give me guidance without pretense
My spiritual existence exudes the rare shades
of the rainbow because my beauty shines bright
My success is measured by my accomplished deeds
day and night
I rise with courage of mind, body and soul
to achieve my goals
I celebrate my growth as in Nikki Giovanni's poem "Ego
Tripping" my African roots are powerful, forever ready
I keep on ticking
Extraordinary you may conclude, pearls of wisdom are the
treasurers I behold, my rite of passage is earned
and my story is told~

I invite you to experience and share this special presentation of my life's work - thus far: my poetry, art, designs, and letters. My distinctive style has been described as mood setting, soothing, exciting, peaceful, romantic, seductive, and inspiring. I claim it all.

The art of love is much greater than the act itself...

Peace and Light.
Norahs

"Norahs Khan writes and moves with her poetry. She is liquid fire, moving, touching, burning, and caressing with words, symbols, and visions. You can't read or listen to her poetry and be still. Something stirs when she advances the pen... something warm... something that filters through the whole soul. Read her... Listen to her... Feel her..."

Warren Oree
Musician, Composer, Producer, Writer

PRAISE OF NORAH KHAN'S WORK

"I really enjoyed Expressions of Love immensely. The card that was done for me [based on the book] was very nicely done. Not only was it pleasing to the eye, it was also pleasing to the heart. My friend was really pleased with it."

Walter Thomas

"A personal and special card was created for me by Norahs. It was beautiful in design and versed with warmth and poignancy. I appreciate the originality and dept of her creations.

I. Wynette Milliner

"Norahs' poetry represents the true standard of a black woman's experience of love, emotion, pain, and you… she has brought water to an empty well of sensuous poetry that was needed. A joy to read or listen to."

Kendyck Allen

"After becoming aware of Norah's unique talent of written expressions, I wanted to be one of her first customers."

Janice Green

"If any heart ever had a need to speak, Norahs has the words it should use... Truly a feast for the heart and soul... Buy it, read it, then live it."

Michael Washington

"I welcome you to share these words of accolades. Norahs Khan writes and moves with her poetry. She is liquid fire, moving, touching, burning and caressing with words, symbols and visions.

"You can't read or listen to her poetry and be still. Something stirs when she advances the pen, something warm, something that filters through the whole soul.

"Read her, listen to her, feel her.

Warren Oree
Musician, Composer, Producer, Writer

"My husband and I had an amazing time at your boutique. Everything about you screams, "WELCOME". You have a beautiful aura/energy! If we didn't have to get back to Ohio, I would have spent another two hours trying on your wonderful creations. ……I love all of the things I purchased. I cannot wait to get the rest of my 'WEARABLE ART'. Having clothes made just for my curves and height is a real treat. I thank you for your Talent and Spirit."

RHONDA

"I'm not one for unsolicited endorsements; however, Norahs Khan is a brilliant designer! Her designs are aesthetically pleasing to the eye; bold, elegant and sophisticated, while still playful. She puts the 'Woman' back into women's design. In fact, women of color on Hollywood's red carpets are in dire need of Khan's genius, yet women of all walks of life can instantly feel like queens wearing her creations – radiant, regal.

"I'd like to think I know a bit about beauty; I've been pursuing it my entire life, like a child chasing butterflies in an open field, and I must say, the designs of Norahs Khan are as beautiful as they are distinctive. It's her eye; her inner vision; her artistic marriage and exacting balance of grace, elegance and sensuality of the female form that make her designs sing – yes; like Chaka Khan's 'I'm Every Woman.' Imagine Chaka, Natalie Cole, Beyonce' and Michelle Obama in Norahs designs; they're immediately transformed into living art. Picture Iman, Tyra, Naomi and Beverly in Norahs Khan's.

I've stood in the halls of the L'Ouvre in Paris, France and studied De Vinci's, Mona Lisa and can only wonder now; had she been wearing Norahs Khan, she may have smiled. Peace, love and beauty!"

Miles Jaye

Just wanted to drop you a quick line to share how amazing your art makes me feel. I decided to wear the sweater duster (the deep red and black one) paired with a base of black slacks and a black turtleneck to travel to NYC yesterday. I wanted to look elegant but be comfortable given that I was traveling to the US style capital. I felt like a sexy diva and looked like a queen. I got admiring stares and compliments from strangers, family and friends alike–and got the ultimate approval from my gay male cousin who told me I looked divine!!!

"Thanks again for creating such beautiful masterpieces!!!!!"

Mardell N. Artis

[Caption under pictures of customer Angie Stevens] "National recording artist Kurt Carr & me! Girl they was loving my distinctive hand designs, I'm gonna need more! I'm just saying & the earrings set it off even more!

Distinctive, sensual, unique, spirit filled, anointed!!! Norahs Khan wearable art is inspirational and truly divine. From the eyes of the beholder only God our creator could have mastered this special gift that he has blessed Norah with. Your talent and inner spirit speaks volumes in everything you lay your hands on!! Thank you!!

"The World's best kept secret, Norahs Khan wearable art. I'M JUST SAYING!!!"

Angie Stevens

"Ms. Norah's clothing collection transforms every person that wears any of her pieces. When you shop with her, the atmosphere is so soothing. She provides refreshments while you leisurely shop the vast collection. You have the freedom to take your time and feel the spirit of the clothing while gazing at yourself in full length mirrors. I receive compliments every time I wear a piece from her collection. I can go on and on but you must experience it for yourself! Thanks Ms. Norah!"

Lenita Madden

"I had the opportunity to indulge in a bath using Norahs' handmade lavender soap bar and I am officially in love. Not only are the bars beautiful, the aroma carries yet doesn't pull moisture from the skin. Norahs Khan is my new favorite designer and I'm looking forward to jazzing up my style for my 30's."

Dina

"Even my husband said I looked pretty. He never really compliments me. Got a lot "I like your outfit."

SB

"I had the pleasure of wearing one your Distinctive Wearable Art designs while shooting a television commercial in the country of CHINA this past summer!

"The television producers wanted something bright and colorful and I had just the right thing! I have several pieces that you have designed and I get compliments each time I wear them! I travel quite a bit and I love the "easy -wear", non complicated styles. I can just put them on and go!!! I can also change the look of the outfits with ease. "Thank you for making fashion, style, and great taste so affordable and so easy!"

Soneta Malit

"Thanks Norahs for the Mother's Day baskets. I purchased the baskets for six special people in my life and I knew they would appreciate the sensual embrace one can give to self. I told you I felt like loving myself after using your products. I have absolutely no idea how you come up with which ingredients to mix into your products, but honey you have it going on!! I really appreciated the baskets, they arrived on time, they were wrapped perfectly, they all smelled awesome and I could tell they were all prepared with "Love". Each individual told me they would make sure the first experience would be when they were able to honor themselves. My husband, if I may, waits to see what scent I will have on when I come to bed, so, you know what that means, new order. I have to mix things up. Ladies, Ladies, Ladies, honor your bodies and others will to."

Rachelle Washington

"Luxurious Body Products! I recently purchased a set of Honor Your Body products by Norahs. Let me tell you, as soon as I opened the package I knew I was in for a treat. The fragrance was so fantastic I couldn't wait to bathe in it. The soap was so beautifully made. It had real chunks of Shea butter inside. It left my body feeling clean and fresh. After my shower I applied the body butter in the same fragrance, "Summer." It made my body feel soft and luxurious. The scent was just right. Sweet and fragrant but not overpowering. Thank you, Norahs, I can't wait to try your next beautiful Honor Your Body creation!"

Willette

An awesome declaration of oneself through visual and musical perception. Yours truly a supporter forever. Many peace and blessings to be bestowed upon you continuously both now and in the afterlife. I am so proud of you and the masses will be defined with your vision of beauty in the absolute.

Love ya girl!! Dot